Homesteading Animals: Rearing Rabbits For Meat & Fur

Includes Rabbit, Duck & Game Recipes For The Slow Cooker

By

Norman J Stone

Guest Blogger on www.planterspost.com

Published By

www.deanburnpublications

ISBN-13: 978-1500415679

2nd Print October 2014

Acknowledgements/ Recommended Reading

A special thanks to F. A. Paris for the game recipes obtained from 'Slow Cooking Heaven' (Copied by Permission)

<u>Slow Cooking Heaven</u> by F. A. Paris

<u>Modern Homesteading</u> 5 Book Bundle by Norman J Stone

Other Books In The Homesteading Animals Series:

<u>Homesteading Animals (2) – Delightful Ducks</u>

<u>Homesteading Animals (3) - Gourmet Geese</u>

<u>Homesteading Animals (4) - Raising Chickens</u>

Table of Contents

Contents

Why Keep Rabbits? 6
Introduction: 9
Glossary of Terms: 12
Choosing Your Rabbits: 17
Popular Rabbit Breeds 18
    American Chinchilla: 18
    American Sable: 19
    Cinnamons: 20
    Californian: 21
    Flemish Giant: 22
    French Angora: 23
    New Zealand White: 25
    Rex Rabbit: 26
Rabbit Care 27
Costs & Considerations! 30
    Start-Up Costs: 33
    Production Expectations: 35
    Commercial Choices: 38
Breeding: 41
Killing & Butchering 43
Preparing Pelts 48

Authors Note: 50

Tasty Rabbit, Duck & Game Recipes 52

    Rabbit & Red Wine Stew 52

    Pheasant with Cherries 54

    Pheasant with Pancetta & Sweet Chestnuts 56

    Venison & Cranberry Stew 58

    Duck Breast in Orange Sauce 60

Acknowledgements/ Recommended Reading 61

Copyright

Copyright © 2014, Norman J Stone

All rights reserved. Copyright protected. Duplicating, reprinting or distributing this material without the express written consent of the author is prohibited.

The information contained in this book is for general advice only. The statements contained herein have not been evaluated nor approved by the US Food & Drug administration.

While reasonable attempts have been made to assure the accuracy of the information contained within this publication, the author does not assume any responsibility for errors, omissions or contrary interpretation of this information, and any damages incurred by that.

The author does not assume any responsibility or liability whatsoever, for what you choose to do with this information.

The cooking and other techniques described in this publication are for your general guidance only.
Use your own judgment.

**

Why Keep Rabbits?

I suppose the quick answer to this question would be – why not! For the fact is, that Rabbit is one of the cheapest, most nutritional; and 'good for you' meats available in the market-place today.

For the homesteader, or indeed anyone with space for a simple rabbit hutch or enclosure; the rabbit is cheap to buy, produces a very lean meat which is high in protein, low in fat and has less than half the calories of Pork. Rabbits are easy to rear and breed, and make considerably less noise that chickens or geese!

They are super-efficient convertors; pound for pound, a rabbit produces 6 times more meat per food and water intake, than a full grown cow!

Check out the following chart to compare rabbit with other popular meat sources.

Common Nutrition Values:

Meat Type	% Protein	% Fat	Calories Per Lb
Rabbit	20.8	4.5	795
Beef	16.7	28.0	1,440
lamb	15.7	27.7	1,420
Chicken	20.0	17.9	810
Pork	11.9	45.0	2,050
Duck	16.0	28.6	1,015
Turkey	20.1	20.0	1,190

Quite apart from the meat, there is also the fur or pelts to consider. Whilst this is pretty much dependent on the breed of rabbit you intend to keep, the pelts can be sold on to help make a few extra dollars for feedstuffs etc – quite apart from whatever you may decide to make with them, such as pocket warmers, glove collars, warm liners for boots etc…More on what you can do with Rabbit pelts, later in this book.

For anyone involved with Homesteading or Hobby-farming, then I hope to help convince you through this short introduction, that rabbits are indeed worth considering when it comes to self-sustainability issues, and feeding the family with top quality, home grown products.

Just as is the case with all types of poultry farming, breeding rabbits can have a major impact when it comes to stocking the food larder, and is also a great way to introduce the idea of Homesteading values to the kids!

As a youngster, one of my first jobs was to look after the rabbits, and thereby gain invaluable knowledge in the years to come regarding the rearing and general care of several species of domestic animals.

It was an excellent grounding in the whole area of self-sustainability, and something I have never regretted learning over the years since – though I do remember hating it at the time, when my friends were off enjoying the football and I was cleaning out rabbit cages!

Introduction:

Rabbit is in my opinion, one of the most underestimated and ignored source of food available in the market place today. The reasons are numerous, but go as far back as the film 'Watership Down' in 1978, when children the world over were lulled into the whole idea of the 'cute bunny rabbit' and went around singing 'Bright eyes, burning like fire, bright eyes……' Yea, call me cynical, but that is where it all went wrong!

The UK in particular went rabbit crazy, and any idea of treating rabbit as a food source went right out the window! Strangely enough, this 'corruption' did not seem to hit Europe in general, as much as it did the UK and the USA. Rural France in particular, has always seen rabbits and even guinea pigs as an excellent cheap, but highly nutritional food source – and rightly so.

Another big reason to my mind, for this move away from the livestock yard to the pets cage, was the introduction of Myxomatosis (Myxy). First discovered in Uruguay at the end of the 19th century, it was introduced to Australia in 1950; and in 1952 introduced almost by accident into France by the bacteriologist Dr. Paul Armand Delille – while trying to control the rabbits on his private estate.

The virus quickly spread throughout France, wiping out some 90% of the rabbit population; before spreading out through-out the rest of Europe. By 1955 95% of the UK rabbit population suffered the same fate; and the disease/virus is now spread throughout the United States and South America.

In all examples the results were devastating to the rabbit populations, and in different ways contributed to the lack of interest in many quarters today with regards to rabbits as a genuine food source.

There were several reasons for the demise of the rabbit from our butcher shop windows.

Firstly: The fact that many children were now keeping rabbits as pets, resulted in them growing up to consider them as just that. This meant that to kill and eat their rabbit's would be tantamount to killing and eating their dog or cat!

First lesson in keeping animals for meat – never give them a name! To do so is to personalise them, and make it difficult – even for adults- to consider killing them for meat. Naming something gives it personality, and makes it many times more difficult when the day comes to introduce them as guest of honour at the dinner table!

Secondly: I don't know if you have ever seen a rabbit with Myxomatosis? If not, then believe me it is not a pretty sight. The first signs of a rabbit with Myxy, is usually the fact that they do not run away from you. This is because the swelling and discharge from their eyes makes them blind, whilst the virus causes them to stumble around as if drunk.

It is indeed a pitiful sight, and would put anyone off the idea of eating rabbit should they come across one infected by this hideous virus – even though the disease cannot be transmitted to humans, making the rabbit itself fit for consumption…hmmm.

Thirdly: Simple economics have played their own part in the demise of rabbit from our dinner tables. With the loss of supply exacerbated by the myxy, coupled with the reluctance of breeders to breed something that no-one wants; the sight of rabbit hanging in the butchers window became something of a rarity – meaning that fewer and fewer children grew up with the idea that rabbit was indeed on the menu!

Thankfully however, things seem to be on the turn again, and interest in rabbit as a good nutritional food source is growing along with the general interest in healthy home-grown food.

Rabbits are once again adorning my local butchers shop window, and whilst it may still be something of a novelty in some areas, people are finally awakening to the nutritional value of this much-ignored food source.

Hopefully this trend will continue, and offer a welcome financial as well as material boost to any Homesteader, who is keen to learn all about rearing rabbits for profit as well as for meat and fur.

Glossary of Terms:

Listed below is a selection of the common terms used amongst rabbit breeders.

Adult: A mature rabbit of breeding age, usually 6 months and older.

Albino: A rabbit with white fur and pink eyes.

Alter: A rabbit that has been spayed (female) or neutered (male).

ARBA: American Rabbit Breeders Association.

Arch: A term used to describe a gentle curvature of the spine on rabbits.

Awn fluff: The soft intermediate downy hairs that end with a straight tip.

Awn hair: The strong straight guard-hair on the rabbit.

Back: The back of the rabbit from head to tail.

Bangs: The longer wool generally found at the base of the ears or atop the head.

Barn: Another name given to a rabbit hutches kept together in a purpose built building.

Base color: The color of the coat next to the skin.

Bell ears: Rabbit ears that have a distinctive tip and fall.

Belly: The underside of the rabbit from the front to the back.

Belt: The line where the colored portion of the hair meets the white, just behind the shoulders.

BEW: A short term for Blue Eyed White rabbit.

Binky: What an excited rabbit does when it jumps up in the air and kicks its legs out, while standing still or running.

Bloodline: A term to denote the pedigree of the rabbit.

Bloom: The finish and vitality of the rabbits coat when in excellent condition.

BOB: In shows this denotes Best of Breed.

Boils: An infection causing boils in the skin.

Bonding: Rabbits that have paired up to form an inseparable bond.

BRC: British Rabbit Council.

Breeder: An individual who breeds rabbits, or used to describe a rabbit that is used primarily for breeding purposes.

Broken coat: A coat that has been affected by moulting, or one that has the guard hairs missing in places.

Buck: An intact male rabbit able to breed.

Buck teeth: A situation where the incisors meet together instead of the top incisors overlapping the bottom. Also called pegged teeth.

Bunny Burrito: A rabbit wrapped tightly in a towel in order to administer medication.

Caked teats: A does mammary glands engorged with milk.

Cannibalism: A doe eating her own young (usually a sign of stress).

Cecotrope Pellet: The soft pellet that is eaten straight from the anus.

Cobby: A stocky short body type.

Coprophagy: The normal practice of eating some droppings straight from the anus.

Cecum: The biggest part of the GI tract in the rabbit, where the food gets processed.

Chinning: A term used to describe the habit whereby a rabbit will rub its chin (where it has scent glands), on objects it wishes to make a claim upon.

Circling: The act just before mating where rabbits will run around in circles chasing each other.

Cross-breeding: Breeding individuals of different species.

Culling: The selective process where rabbits will be killed for commercial or other reasons.

Dam: Female that has produced a litter. A rabbits dam would be its mother.

Dew claw: An extraneous claw on the inside of the leg.

Dewlap: The skin that hangs under the chin of the female rabbit, used to pluck wool for nesting.

Doe: Female rabbit.

Dressing: Preparing an animal for the table.

Ear canker: A condition of the ear causing inflammation and general discomfort. Caused by rabbit ear mites.

Flank: The side of the rabbit above the belly between the ribs and the hips.

Fryer: A young rabbit between 3 and 5 pounds in weight.

Gestation: The time between mating and kindling of a female.

Guard hair: The longer coarser hair protecting the rabbits coat.

Hindquarters: The rear-end of the rabbit consisting of loins, hips, rump and hind legs.

Hock: The middle joint of the hind leg between the joint and the foot.

In Kimble: Pregnant rabbit.

Kindling: The process of giving birth.

Kindling box: Nest box for the rabbit.

Kit: A baby rabbit.

Litter: Young rabbits.

Malocclusion: The misalignment of teeth.

Moult: The process where a rabbit loses hair or the old coat.

Mounting: Rabbits will mount each other to show who is the boss. Not related to sexual or mating behaviour.

Muzzle: The projecting part of the face including the mouth, nose, and lower jaw.

Myxomatosis: A fatal disease introduced over 50 years ago to control rabbit populations.

Open Doe: A rabbit of breeding age not yet having bred.

Out breeding: The mating of unrelated rabbits.

Palpate: A way to check for pregnancy by feeling the abdominal wall.

Quad: A group of rabbits put together for breeding purposes.

Rabbit fever: An infection in rabbits caused by the bacterium Francisella tularensis. Transferable to humans by contact with infected animals or ticks.

Roughage: Grass, hay, or other similar semi-dry organic material consumed by rabbits.

Sexing: The process of checking out a rabbits genitals to determine its sex.

Sire: Male rabbit that has produced offspring.

Succulent feed: Soft green grass or vegetation.

Suckling period: The time that a kit feeds from its mother.

Thumping: When a rabbit is afraid or warning of danger, it will thump the ground with its hind legs.

Vent disease: Found in both sexes, this is indicated by a red, inflamed or scabby male and female organs.

Viral Haemorrhagic Disease: Usually fatal disease to any rabbit unfortunate enough to catch it – similar in this respect to Myxomatosis.

Weaning: The time when the kits are removed from the doe, to signify the end of the nursing period.

Wool block: A blockage of the digestive tract caused by a wool mass.

Choosing Your Rabbits:

There are many domestic rabbit breeds to choose from, when considering the best ones for meat. Listed here is a selection of the most popular, along with their particular specifications.

Be aware also that you do not choose the wrong animal for your particular climate. The French Angola for instance, with its warm woolly coat, would not do well in the Arizona sunshine! A little research before purchase of a particular breed is always recommended.

As for the rabbits themselves; always give new stock a good check over to see that they are fit and healthy for breeding.

Things to check for instance is inside the ears – make sure that there are no signs of scabbing, caused by ear mites. Its nose should be dry and free from running or crusting. Hocks and feet should be free of any sore spots, and eyes clear and free from discharge of any kind.

Carefully inspect the fur for any signs of fleas or other vermin, this can be a major factor in the spread of disease, and indeed it is how Myxomatosis itself is spread amongst the rabbit population.

As an added precaution, I would always apply a period of quarantine before presenting any new rabbit to my rabbitry, just in case there is some disease that has not yet revealed itself in outward appearance.

Finally, always buy from a reputable dealer or someone that you know breeds good rabbits if at all possible; at least that way you will have some sort of guarantee that the animal is healthy and a good specimen.

Popular Rabbit Breeds

There is a virtually unlimited choice when it comes to rabbit breeds, especially if you are not averse to cross bred rabbits. Here are a few of the more popular breeds to consider when choosing rabbits for your homestead.

American Chinchilla:

Originating in France, and introduced to America in 1919; this popular 'heavyweight' is bred for its meat as well as thick pelt. The American Chinchilla has been bred especially for its meat and fur, and weighs in at between 12-16lbs. It is of a docile temperament, and is often a favourite of the children as a family pet.

American Sable:

Bred from the Chinchilla rabbit, the American Sable is a medium sized animal with the bucks averaging around 7-9 lbs and the does weighing 8-10 lbs.

A popular breed with a docile nature, it is very popular for its dense Sable colour coat. Almost extinct back in the 1980's, it was brought back 'to life' by the dedicated efforts of Ohio breeder, Al Roerdanz.

Cinnamons:

A medium sized rabbit weighing around 9lbs, the Cinnamon is characterized by its striking coloured fur. Cinnamon or rust covered back, with Smokey grey sides and dark underbelly; an orange under-colouring gives a unique look to this impressive looking (and tasting!) animal.

Californian:

Developed in the 1920's by George West in California; this rabbit is one of the larger varieties, weighing around 12lbs. Striking white coat with black ears, feet, nose, and tail; this particular breed can be a little troublesome inasmuch as they do not tolerate extremes of temperature, and are prone to hairball obstructions – particularly if care is not taken with their grooming.

Flemish Giant:

First recognised as a breed in 1893, the Flemish Giant is as its name suggests - an enormous animal; weighing anything up to and over 20lbs. It is known as an extremely docile creature, and is soon well adapted to regular handling. A popular breed at rabbit shows; it comes in a variety of colours including black, blue, fawn, light grey, sandy, steel grey and white.

Very popular for meat and fur, as well as a show animal.

French Angora:

Bred mainly for their fur – At only 11 microns in diameter it is finer and softer than cashmere - The French Angora rabbit was popular amongst the French court in the mid-18th century. Distinguishable from the English Angora by the lack of fur on the face and ears, the French Angora's coat is confined to its body.

Although reared for meat (7.5 to 10lbs) as well as wool, it is also an excellent choice of breed for showing – although it does take a fair amount of maintenance to keep the coat in good condition.

New Zealand White:

A popular rabbit for both meat and fur, the New Zealand White has a large, broad body, and grows to about 9.5 lbs for the male and a slighter heavier 10-12 lbs for the female.

This is a very popular breed for both its meat and the excellent quality fur; which is used for fur coats and trimmings.

Rex Rabbit:

Another popular breed for both meat and fur, the Rex is also known as being one of the most intelligent of the rabbit breeds – even known to perform tricks on command!

Weighing in at around 10lbs; it is very compliable and easy to manage.
It is also very able to cope with changing temperatures, and is often kept outside summer and winter with no problems.

Rabbit Care

Just like any other animal (or vegetable for that matter), rabbits have to be properly cared for in order to get the best results. Even from a humanitarian point of view, it is important to **treat any animal in your care with respect** and give it the best life possible before it 'reaches the table' – if indeed that it where it is destined.

With that in mind, here are a few tips regarding the basic living conditions and feed necessary for successful rabbit breeding.

Feeding:

Rabbits are fairly simple to feed, and there are many commercial feedstuffs on the market today, including pellets and dry mash. However a large part of the diet should consist of good quality hay (around 70% ideally), which provides much needed roughage to the diet. Timothy hay or meadow hay is best.

Rabbits love lettuce – NEVER feed it to them! It contains lactucarium which causes diarrhoea, and has been known to cause GI Stasis, a fatal condition.

I usually supplement these commercial feeds with vegetables, grass, or even weeds pulled from my garden – just be sure there is nothing poisonous amongst the selection like eggplants, potato plants, tomato or buttercup leaves – to name just a very few!

Even parsnip, which contains Psoralens, is poisonous to rabbits. If in any doubt, just don't feed it to them! With that said, there is an abundance of information on the internet regarding plants poisonous to rabbits.

Cages/Hutch:

The size of cage needed to keep your rabbits, does vary according to the breed you are keeping; however as a general rule of thumb, a rabbit needs around 4 times its body size to give enough space to move around. It should also be high enough for it to stand on its hind legs.

Wire mesh should be strong quality and small enough to prevent the rabbit (including young) to get stuck in it, as well as escaping – particularly if used on the base as mesh the wrong size will hurt their feet.

The habitat should include an ample clean water supply, a litter box, and hay for bedding. If the cage does have a wire mesh bottom, give the rabbit a flat area to stand on and avoid foot discomfort/damage.

Include a 'run' if possible, to enable a little freedom and exercise for the rabbit. If the rabbits are to be kept outdoors, make sure that they have good protection from the elements, and are not harassed by predators such as dogs or foxes – remember happy bunnies are productive bunnies!

Cleaning:

Clean the cage regularly – at least twice per week, for a 'deep clean,' where you should scrub down the toilet area or litter box particularly, with a suitable cleaner, (Vinegar is an excellent choice for this). Be careful using strong detergent, as it may react with the waste and produce strong ammonia fumes! A bleach solution of 1 part bleach to ten parts water is ideal for this.

On a daily basis, the cage should be cleared of any half-chewed or uneaten vegetable matter, water dish cleaned out and filled with fresh water, and fresh hay installed.

A quick inspection for any creepy-crawlies such as lice, fleas or ticks is always a good thing!

Use an old tub or basin to clean anything relating to your rabbits – NEVER the kitchen sink!

Costs & Considerations!

As with any project, there are a lot of things to consider when thinking of rearing rabbits. Cost is almost (but not always) the major consideration, and by that I mean not only the cost of the rabbit and the feed, but also the general start-up cost inherent with any new project.

You may be planning to raise just enough rabbits to provide the family with a source of quality meat, or you may be considering operating a more commercial rabbitry with emphasis on the profits to be made.

There are several ways to profit from breeding rabbits including the following.

1: Selling directly to individuals, both for meat or just as pets.

2: Selling the dressed rabbits directly to restaurants or game dealers.

3: Deal through a 'middle-man' who will take the hassle of dressing and dealing with individual shops from you – at a cost!

4: Selling the pelts to businesses using rabbit fur to adorn their products.

5: Monies saved through NOT buying meat from the store must be included as profit.

6: Rabbit droppings make great compost – sell it to keen gardeners!

Pros and Cons!

Here is a short list of 'pros' and 'cons' to think about when contemplating your own rabbitry business.

Pros:

1: It can provide extra income as well as meat for the family. It Is also great for the kids to see just what is involved in producing the food that is put on the dinner plate!

2: Rabbit meat is exceptionally lean meat, extremely low in fat and lower in calories than chicken. This assures you of a good healthy product to feed the family.

3: You can save money by not having to purchase more expensive meats at the supermarket – that would most likely be less nutritional than rabbit.

4: Rabbits are easier to raise than most other livestock as they require less space, and are easy breeders. Ideal for areas where there is a shortage of land.

5: Rabbits are far less demanding and require less physical work than other animals.

6: Even the rabbit manure has a value as it can be sold to wormeries or directly to gardeners, as it makes excellent compost.

7: Very productive. An average NZW can produce around 200lbs of meat in a single year if conditions are right.

8: Rabbit skins, especially the white breeds, are in demand from fashion houses and other commercial outlets.

Cons:

1: If starting from scratch, the initial outlay can be fairly costly with regard to breeding stock, cages and other requirements. More on this below.

2: The food consumer in general is not so aware of the benefits to be gained from eating rabbit meat, therefore a ready market for your product may need some work.

3: Rabbit care for the beginner can be difficult to begin with, especially if profit is the main consideration. Only hands-on experience over time will improve your rabbit production and profitability.

4: Although not hard work, the rabbits nevertheless have to be attended daily, which means that there is not a lot of 'me time.'

***

After considering the pros and cons of raising rabbits, the other obvious questions are how much? And what should I expect in respect to meat production?

Listed in the next chapter you will find a brief outline of the costs, and what you may expect in terms of production.

Start-Up Costs:

Costing your enterprise does depend a lot on where you stay, as does the relative value of your produce. Things such as sheds, wire netting, feed, nest boxes, along with your stock of rabbits will vary – especially the different rabbit breeds you may choose.

Here though is a rough idea of where you may expect your costs and production levels to be as a newbie rabbit breeder.

Taking the New Zealand White as an example, the figures below are an approximation of what you may expect regarding production rates and costs.

Rabbits: Good quality NZW will usually cost around $50 each. As you may expect it is usually best to go for the more expensive if that is best quality.

Feed: The average cost for a 50lb bag of rabbit feed is usually around $15.

Hutch Heaters: You may well need heaters depending of course on your location. Rabbits are very hardy animals but you may well need a heater to prevent water from freezing. An oil-filled radiator should cost about $50 depending of course on type and output.

Cooling Fan: Rabbits do not perform well in excessive heat, and can easily be put off breeding and even expire if the temperature goes above 90F in the hut. Bucks can also go sterile in a hot environment. $30 should cover the cost of a good fan.

Hay: Rabbits need plenty of roughage in their diet to help their digestive system and a good quality hay will do the trick just fine. A bale of hay will cost around $5 depending on the supply.

New Cages: You can of course make your own cages if you are able, but a cage 18" tall by 30" deep and 36" wide would usually cost around $40 each.

Nest Boxes (metal): Metal boxes are preferable for sanitary purposes, and also because the rabbits cannot chew them. These will usually cost around $20.

Feed Dispensers: Large metal feeders are best as they need less filling and they cannot be chewed. Expected cost is around $7.

Water Dispensers: Avoid open bowls or troughs as they will soon become insanitary. Choose instead brass nipple feeders or water bottle dispensers at around $6 each.

Costs Breakdown:

Rabbits (4) 1 Buck 3 Does...............$ 200
Feed (I bag)...................................$15
Heaters (1).....................................$50
Cooling Fan (1).............................$30
Hay (1 bale)....................................$5
Cages ($40 x 7 for grow-out) $280
Nest Boxes (3)...............................$60
Feed Dispensers x 7........................$49
Water Dispensers x 7......................$42
Misc buckets, shovels, cleaning equip.....$50

Grand Total................................$781

You may well incur other costs on top of this, or indeed save some costs by DIY effort. However this at least will give you some idea of what exactly may be involved.

On-going expenses especially with regard to feed, will depend on the amount of rabbits being catered for.

One other big expense you may have here is a shed or other structure to house your rabbits.

Production Expectations:

What about Production?

Notwithstanding the achievable weights of the different animals listed before-hand, rabbits bred for sale art at their best at the 'Fryer' stage – which is generally between 9-11 weeks.

This is when the meat is at the most tender, and is calculated as being the most cost-effective stage with regard to food consumed versus weight gained.

However you may well have a market for allowing the animal to grow to its maximum weight, in order to get a better weight-per-pound price.

For the sake of this work however, he following calculations are taken on the basis that the kits are reared to the Fryer stage before sale.

Listed below is an approximation of what you may expect from 3 Does and 1 Buck over the course of 1 year, with respect to offspring and meat produced.

These figures are based on a series of assumptions to give us a figure that will not be far from the actual numbers achieved.

Does can be presented to the Buck in as little as 14 days after kindling. This would achieve 8 litters per year. For these figures however I have assumed a 21 day period after kindling, which should achieve 7 litters per year.

At 8 kits per litter this will give you 56 kits per Doe, meaning around 168 offspring per year from 3 Does.

The fryers should achieve the premium killing weight of 5.5lbs in about 8-10 weeks. Of this, some 3.25lbs of actual meat can be processed.

This basically means that one Doe can produce around 182lbs per year with 7 litters or 208lbs at 8 litters.

Bear in mind that this is an 'Ideal World' scenario. In real life you will have to make allowances for different sizes of litters, as well as mortality rates – where there is Livestock, there is Deadstock!

'Guestimated' Annual Costs:

The annual costs over the year of producing all these rabbits should be around **$1,080.00**

This is **NOT** taking into consideration the start-up costs looked at earlier, as apart from the feed calculation included in the list, this will not be an annual cost

How to calculate feed? This is not an exact science, but it will do for our purposes at this time. The best way to do this is to say that a kit, from birth to market-weight will consume around 3.5lbs of feed for every 1lb of weight gained.

If we consider that killing weight of 5.5lbs. This means that a kit will consume 19.25lbs of feed to reach the Fryer weight of 5.5lbs.

Over the course of the year the 56 kits produced will consume around 1,071 lbs of meal + hay + adult feed.

We could safely say around **1100lbs of feed + hay and water** for 1 adult and kits over the year.

This should come in at around $330 for feed, and around $30 for hay.

This gives a total feed cost for 1 Doe of around $360 for the year to raise 182lbs of meat at 7 litters per Doe.

Annual Calculations for raising 168 kits from 3 Does:

Total Feed Cost = $1,080.00

Feed Consumed = 3300 lbs

Fryers produced (7 litter calc) = 168

Pounds of meat produced at 3.25lb per fryer = 546lbs

Cost of Meat Produced = $1.97 per lb.

Commercial Choices:

Selling via a Middleman:

This is the 'quick fix' way to sell your rabbits, whereby you just hand over the complete rabbit to someone who will then prepare it for retail use and sell it on.

If you consider that a commercial 'Middle man' will pay anything between $1.25 and $2.00 per pound for the complete rabbit, there is not much margin (if anything) for error if you are breeding commercially and hope to make a profit.

Selling Direct to public:

However if you are able to comply with local authority food-handling regulations and dress the meat yourself to retail directly to the public, then things get a little more interesting.

Prepared or dressed rabbit meat retails at anything between $7 and $10 **per pound** for a whole Fryer – usually weighing only 3-4 lbs. This would value your 5.5 lb fryer at between $38.5 and $70.00 !

If you add the value of the rabbit pelts and rabbit manure (which is not a lot but it all adds up), then this could be a very profitable commercial exercise.

Selling To Trade:

Similarly selling prepared rabbit to trade retailers, means having to comply with regulations and food standards for public health and safety reasons.

However if you can manage this then a large retailer is able to take significant amounts of stock at any one time, and will usually enter into a long-term contract with you.

Of course they must get their cut, as they are in it like you – for the profit! This is when you must be able to negotiate a price that you are both happy with, and that is usually based around your bottom line (how much you must make to make the whole exercise profitable enough for your needs); and how much stock they are offering to take from you at any given time.

Obviously the more stock a retail outlet offers to take from you, then the tougher the negotiations become!

Bottom line – anything you get over **your total production costs** is profit, however in the scenario above I would aim to negotiate over $3.50 per pound or $19.25 per Fryer to make it worth-while.

Domestic Consumption:

Of course if you are breeding rabbits for your own consumption, with perhaps a few sales to friends and family, then a lot of what has been mentioned before-hand does not comply.

For instance, your main consideration may simply be the fact that you are producing excellent nutritional meat, for a fraction of what it would cost you in the supermarket. This is a great saving on the family budget, and the overall 'healthy foods' consumption.

Costs can be cut down when breeding limited amounts by supplementing expensive feed-stuffs with organic material like fresh greens from the garden, and perhaps hay that you or a neighbour produces themselves (homesteaders take note!).

You can also get a good income by not killing all the rabbits for food, but by selling some for pets. Prices vary widely according to breed, location etc, but it would be reasonable to expect anything between $25 and $50 per rabbit.

Bottom line is that you may be able to sell enough of the rabbits to pay for the whole batch – meaning that your own consumption is cost-free!

Breeding:

When ready to start breeding your rabbits, always introduce the Doe to the Buck, and never the opposite way around. Does can very protective of their 'space' and will often attack any Buck that you introduce to her.

Doe's are always ready to breed, so as soon as you introduce the Buck, he will get right down to business most of the time – perhaps after a brief chase around the cage. When the buck has successfully mated with the doe, he will fall back or to the side. This is usually allowed to happen two or three times, just to be sure, and then they are separated.

This date should be marked on a calendar, and approximately 31 days after, you should have your first litter of up to 8 kits.

Before this happens however, the doe will start to prepare her nest about 14 days after mating. This is achieved by her pulling fur from under her neck and belly, along with clumps of hay, and building her nest – hopefully in a box that you have already provided! Be sure that you have also provided clean, soft hay for the bedding; straw is not advised as it can be a bit 'pointy' and cause damage to the kits eyes.

When the time comes, be sure to give her some peace and quiet, and she will manage just fine – pregnancy is not hard on the female and the birth will usually go without a hitch.

Baby Rabbits (kits)

Young rabbits are born furless with their eyes closed, but develop quickly and can be weaned from their mother (introduced to solid food), at about 5 weeks, though suckling may continue up to 8 weeks.

During the nursing period it is important to leave the rabbits in peace, as a stressed adult my kill or refuse to suckle the young. That said, it is not unusual for a new mother to kill her first litter; but there-after she usually manages just fine.

The mother will only nurse the young once or twice per day, and in-between will leave them to their own devices in the nest – so do not be concerned by her apparent lack of interest if she is standing a short distance from the nest for most of the day.

Rabbits are quick developers, and at 8-10 weeks old they are perfect copies of their parents – this is the ideal time to buy.

Killing & Butchering

This is perhaps the most difficult part of rearing rabbits for the table – especially if you are the least bit squeamish! For myself I have to be honest, I do not like killing things! However the simple fact is that this is part of living on a homestead, and if I were to be overly squeamish then I would be better living in an apartment in the city, and filling myself with pre-processed foods – perish the thought.

So to get to the inevitable part of rearing your animals for food, means that when the time is ripe you must be prepared to kill them – or get some-one to do it for you. At this point I must mention that if you are going to butcher your animals to sell on, then you will most likely have to have the appropriate licence from your local authority to do so.

I will place a link at the end of this book to a particularly effective harvesting tool called 'The Rabbit Wringer' that may help you out, when it comes to dispatching your rabbits cleanly and effectively.

Killing Age?

The ideal age to kill and butcher your rabbits is usually about 10-12 weeks depending on the breed. This usually means in weight around 4-5lbs. Sometimes however a 'Fryer' may be chosen for more tender meat, if it is large enough. (A 'fryer' is a rabbit around 11 weeks old.)

The main point here is that the animal must be killed quickly and humanely - causing the animal to suffer is not acceptable, and indeed will get you into trouble with the law in most countries - nor is it necessary as there are cheap devices on the market today that will do the job cleanly and exceedingly efficiently.

The 'old fashioned' way to kill a rabbit, is simply to hold it by its hind legs; and perform a stiff 'karate chop' to the back of its head. This normally does the job just fine, by breaking the neck.

As mentioned however, there are now several mechanical instruments to dispatch the rabbits that involve electrical stunning, shooting or breaking the neck either manually or via an instrument such as the 'Rabbit Wringer.' This is simply fixed in position and the rabbit is inserted and pulled to achieve a quick kill.

Skinning:

Once the rabbit is humanely dispatched, you then have to remove the pelt. This is done in 5 easy steps.

1: Hang up the rabbit by the hind legs, and cut carefully around the leg just above the joint. Cut just to the depth of the skin itself and not deep into the flesh.

2: Cut from that slice on each leg, down to the anus of the animal, and carefully peel away the skin from the bone, down to the tail.

3: Remove the tail piece by cutting away the small bone. Be careful not to pierce the bladder at this point.

4: Take both hands and gently pull the pelt away from the body, remove the skin from the front legs as you go and pull all the way down to the head.

5: Remove the head and feet with a sharp knife or heavy shears, then pull the skin completely away from the carcase.

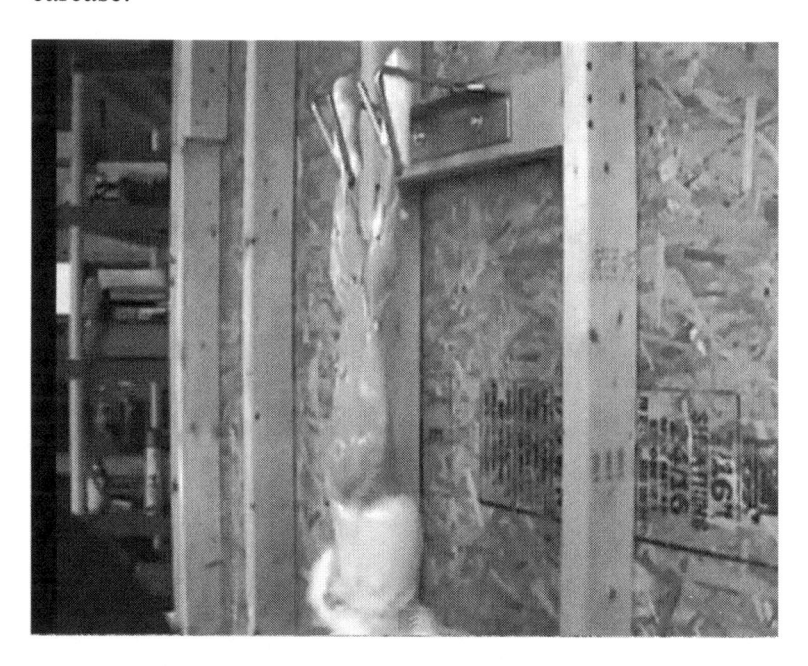

Cleaning The Carcase:

With the pelt removed it is now time to clean or 'dress' the carcase, this can be done by leaving the rabbit hanging where it is, and providing a bowl or receptacle to receive the guts and waste material.

With the rabbit still hanging above the receptacle, make an insertion at the groin, and carefully slip your knife down through the length of the belly. Be careful to cut just the depth of the flesh, and not to cut into the guts (especially the gall bladder which is attached to the liver - a small thing about the size of a pea).

Pull out the guts, then remove the liver and kidneys from the cavity. Cut through the rib cage then remove the heart and lungs.

Finally clean the rabbit in fresh water, and let it rest in a fridge for 6-24 hours before use.

Butchering/Boning:

1: Lay the carcase on its back and split the rib-cage down the breastbone with a sharp pair of shears.

2: Laying the rabbit on its side, hold one of the hind legs and cut around to separate it from the body. Repeat with other leg.

3: Where the backbone meets the pelvis, slice through and twist to separate and detach the pelvis area from the main body.

4: Starting at the top of the ribcage, slip your knife down each side to separate the ribs from the body. Detach the loin that runs along the backbone.

5: Use you sharp knife to detach the more deeply set ribs one by one.

6: With the rear of the rabbit facing you, cut away the ribcage to butterfly the tenderloin.

7: Reverse the rabbit and slip your knife under the backbone, and gently ease your knife up the spine to remove it from the rabbit, pulling with the other hand to help separate it.

This will leave you with a boned rabbit, ready to cut into pieces and cook as per your recipe.

Alternatively you can go 'rustic' and after trimming away any excess fat, sinew or silverskin (the thin silvery membrane that covers the body) simply cut the rabbit into six pieces – two rear legs, two front and the loin or 'saddle' cut into two pieces.

Add to the slow cooker, and follow the recipe below for Rabbit & Red wine stew!

Preparing Pelts

Once the pelt has been removed from the animal, then it is time to prepare it for tanning. This is a process whereby the hide can be preserved to make it more pliable, enduring and resistant to water and decay.

Once a hide has been properly tanned or cured, then it can be used to make anything from fur coats to linking boots or gloves. It is also a popular material for lining the cuffs of jackets.

Tanning hides can also be an important part of any rabbit breeders income, as the French Angora rabbit for instance has a beautiful coat that can adapted for many commercial uses in the fashion industry.

There are many ways to tan a hide, and indeed many people will swear by their favourite method. However for now we will just look at the basics of tanning, that will allow you to preserve your pelt; and perhaps prepare it for sale!

Here is a simple tanning method to follow in 8 easy steps. Remember to wear suitable protective gloves!

1. Wash and clean the skin thoroughly, removing any blood or waste material. This is important as any blood left on the hide will stain the leather. Squeeze the pelt dry after this step is completed – do not wring the pelt!

2. Pour two gallons of room-temperature water into a suitable container, then add one cup of course salt (noniodized), and one cup of Alum (can be bought at most hardware/pharmacies or feed stores).

3. After thoroughly mixing the ingredients, add the pelt to the mix (or pickle) and stir around with a wooden spoon. Make sure that the pelt is thoroughly immersed, and leave in the mix for a further 48 hours.

4. Remove the hide from the mix, (keep the mixture for re-use later) and begin the process of 'fleshing.' This is to remove any fatty tissue, and in the case of rabbits is simply done by scraping away or removing the thin under-tissue from the pelt. Once finished, rinse the pelts in clean water and squeeze out excess liquid.

5. Add the same amount of salt and alum mix to your reserved brine, and add your pelts to the liquid, pressing down with the wooden spoon to make sure of proper infusion. Leave for seven days in the brine, stirring gently twice a day.

6. Remove from the brine, and wash with a mild detergent. Finally rinse out the pelts with clean water, and hang to dry in a shady position – NOT in direct sunshine as this will dry out the pelt too quickly, causing it to go brittle.

7. Before the pelt is fully dry, remove from the hanger and work the pelt with your hands to stretch it out and make it supple; this is known as 'breaking up' the pelt. Leave again to dry, then rub some olive oil or massage mink oil into the leather to increase its suppleness.

8. Brush and condition – store in a clean dry space.

This whole process though a bit of work and hassle, will nevertheless produce some excellent results for your pelts, and will make them more valuable and attractive to potential buyers.

Tasty Rabbit, Duck & Game Recipes

First of all, a big thanks to author F. A Paris for allowing the use of these recipes from her Slow Cooker recipe book 'Slow Cooking Heaven' available for kindle download here…

Slow Cooking Heaven Recipe Book

Rabbit & Red Wine Stew

(Serves 6)

Ingredients:

1 Rabbit Jointed & cut into pieces
1 large onion (chopped
1 clove garlic (crushed)
½ pint (0.23 ltr) red wine
¼ pint chicken stock
1 carrot (sliced)
2 oz seeded olives
4 potatoes cut into chunks
2 table spoons plain flower
1 table spoon cooking oil
1/2 oz butter
1 table spoon tomato relish
Salt & ground black pepper to taste

Preparation:

Coat the rabbit pieces in pre-seasoned flour and add to a hot saucepan with the oil and butter. Turn rabbit pieces until browned all over and add to the slow cooker.
Into the saucepan add the onion, garlic, tomato relish stock and red wine. Bring to the boil and simmer for 4-5 minutes. Pour the ingredients into the slow cooker with the rabbit. Add the other ingredients.
Cook on low for 6-8 hours. Taste, and season with salt, and ground black pepper to suit.

Delightful served with a side of boiled potatoes in butter and oatmeal.

*****

Pheasant with Cherries

(Serves 4)

Ingredients:

4 Pheasant breasts
7 oz (198g) shallots halved
1 jar pitted morello cherries
1 large onion (sliced)
2 garlic cloves (crushed)
2 whole cloves
3 bay leaves
1 table spoon honey
½ table spoon mixed spice
1 table spoon brown cane sugar
1/2 pint (0.23 ltr) chicken stock
2 table spoons vegetable oil
½ oz butter
Salt & pepper to taste

Preparation:

Coat the pheasant breasts with well-seasoned flour, and fry with the oil and butter in a saucepan for 4-5 minutes.
Remove and add to the slow cooker.
Add the shallots, garlic and sliced onion to the saucepan and fry for 2-3 minutes, then add the rest of the ingredients.
Bring to the boil and simmer for 4-5 minutes before adding the mix to the slow cooker.
Cook on 'low' for 2 ½ - 3 hours.
Taste, then season/thicken to suit.

Can be served with boiled rice, or potatoes and vegetables, to make an ideal evening meal.

*****

Pheasant with Pancetta & Sweet Chestnuts

(Serves 4)

Ingredients:

4 Pheasant breasts
7 oz (198g) whole peeled chestnuts
7 oz shallots
3 ½ oz (99g) smoked sliced pancetta
1 teaspoon French grainy mustard
2 sliced apples
¼ pint (0.11 ltr) sweet cider
¼ pint chicken stock
1 garlic clove (fine chopped)
1 table spoon tomato relish
2 table spoons plain flour
1 oz butter
Salt & pepper to taste

Preparation:

Dry the pheasant then season well with salt & pepper; wrap the pheasant in the pancetta, holding in place with string or cocktail sticks pierced through the meat. Add to a hot saucepan along with the oil and butter. Fry for 3-4 minutes. Remove and add to the slow cooker.

Into the hot saucepan add the shallots, chestnuts, garlic, stock and the other ingredients. Bring to the boil and simmer for 3-4 minutes, then add to the slow cooker along with the pheasant.

Cook on 'low' for 2 ½ - 3 hours, then season to taste.

Very satisfying dish if served with roast & mashed potatoes & vegetables. Or with a simple base of basmati rice.

*****

Venison & Cranberry Stew

(Serves 4)

Ingredients:

1 lb (450g) venison loin (cubed)
1 onion (chopped)
1 clove garlic (crushed)
5 oz (141g) cranberries
2 oz (56g) mushrooms (sliced)
1 carrot (chopped)
1 table spoon tomato relish
2 sprigs rosemary
1 tsp mixed dried herbs
½ pint (0.23 ltr) brown ale (Guinness?)
¼ pint (0.11ltr) beef stock
2 tsp grainy mustard
2 tsp brown sugar
2 table spoons plain flour
1 table spoon vegetable oil
1 oz butter
Salt & black pepper to season

Preparation:

Coat the diced venison in well-seasoned flour and add to a saucepan with the oil and butter. Fry and turn the meat to brown all sides, then remove and add to the slow cooker.

Add the onion and garlic to the pan and fry for 2-3 minutes, then add the mushrooms, rosemary, mustard, herbs, tomato relish, brown sugar, stock and brown ale to the saucepan. Bring to the boil and simmer for 4-5 mins.
Add the mix to the slow cooker along with the sliced carrots. Add seasoning.
Cook on 'low' for 7-8 hours, taste and season as required.

Fantastic stew for a cold winters evening, served with a creamy mash and green beans.

*****

Duck Breast in Orange Sauce

(Serves 4)

Ingredients:

4 lean duck breasts
3 oranges (sliced)
1 small onion (sliced)
1 garlic clove (fine chopped)
2-3 leaves mint
1 table spoon course marmalade
3/4 pint (0.35 ltr) orange juice
1 table spoon honey
Salt & pepper to taste

Preparation:

Remove any skin from the duck breasts, slice in half and rub over with salt to season.
Layer the duck, onion and oranges in the slow cooker.
Add the orange juice and the rest of the ingredients into a suitable container and mix thoroughly. Pour this mix over the duck in the slow cooker.
Cook on low for 6-8 hours.
When cooked, remove duck and discard the fruit and vegetables, retaining the sauce.
Thicken the sauce to a good consistency with some cornflour or Arrowroot, simmer in a saucepan for 5 minutes or so.

Place duck breasts in a serving dish and pour over the orange sauce.

A delightfully tasty dish served with duck placed on a bed of boiled wild rice. Garnish with slices of Orange.

*****

Authors Note:

I hope you have found this book to be as informative as you expected, and trust that you will put the information in this introductory work to good use!

Homesteading, or simply the desire to live a more sustainable or self-sufficient lifestyle, is becoming of more and more importance as people in general are becoming disenfranchised with the commercialization of every aspect of their lives – and with good reason.

With so many chemical fertilizers promoting rapid fruit and vegetable growth, toxic pest control methods, additives and preservatives added to processed foods to improve the shelf life; it is maybe time we all took a little more control over our food intake at the least!

In this Homesteading series, and the shorter introductions in my Homesteaders K.I.S.S series, I hope to introduce many aspects of self-sustainability – from growing vegetables to rearing a selection of animals synonymous with the Homestead.

Also you can check out my other Homesteading Animals books by clicking on the following links.

Other Books In The Homesteading Series:

Homesteading Animals (2) – Delightful Ducks

Homesteading Animals (3) - Gourmet Geese

Homesteading Animals (4) - Raising Chickens

Finally – A HUGE THANKS for purchasing this book, and if you can spare the time I would really appreciate an honest review of its contents on the Amazon page.

Thanks again,

Norman

***

Acknowledgements/ Recommended Reading

Slow Cooking Heaven by F. A. Paris
Modern Homesteading 5 book Homesteading bundle by author.
www.therabbitwringer.com (Rabbit harvesting equipment)

Made in the USA
Columbia, SC
08 January 2018